Ideas

By Boris Fedorov

Introduction

Whenever I have an idea on a topic I always write it down somewhere so I won't forget about it. Later on I revise these notes to see what ideas are good and which are bad and discuss it with people to get better knowledge.

These are a collection of notes I have on different topics. They are all quite short summarise of beliefs I have for multiple topics, with each section been around 1 page. Some of which I have wrote about before while some have remained as just ideas on paper.

Now that I am able to remember these ideas I will throw away these notes as they have no more purpose however before doing so will publish them in one collected booklet.

The main reason I am publishing these notes, is in order to receive criticism on my philosophy to improve and ultimately achieve a better understanding of the world.

It is also to try and get more people to start thinking about these topics and develop their own philosophy.

I have also left out some of some of my notes on martial arts, computer science, health and teaching. This is because these aspects I am still developing my theories on. The philosophy for those topics is still currently under development and I do not know if it is the best way forward yet. That is why I will first test out my theories on those topics and see if the results are positive and leads to success before publishing as before getting them up for review I think it is important that I am sure that I know these policies will work and will therefore keep those notes as they are still necessary.

You might also notice that I quite often write notes to myself as if I am addressing someone. This is something I do to remember it better and I always want to make my notes readable for anyone so anyone can understand it. So if anyone does read it they can think about the points for themselves, criticise and help others to develop their philosophy as well.

Contents

Core principles...1

  1. Philosophy
  2. Adaptation
  3. Scientific analysis
  4. Criticism
  5. Balance
  6. New Soviet Man

The meaning of life...............................10

  7. Failure
  8. Life and Happiness
  9. Yourself
  10. Determination and never giving up
  11. Adversity
  12. Discipline
  13. Writing to yourself
  14. Actions speak louder than words
  15. Health
  16. Peer pressure
  17. Ego
  18. Self-belief
  19. Knowledge
  20. Death
  21. Decline

Making the world a better place.................27

  22. Empathy

23. Morality
24. Teaching
25. Politics
26. Utopia
27. The transitional face
28. Meritocracy
29. Democracy
30. Helping people
31. Initiative
32. Mass line

Mistaken ideas and correct ideas……………..46

33. Middle man fallacy
34. Existence
35. Time
36. Nostalgia
37. Forgiveness
38. Respect
39. Emotion
40. Control

Different philosophies……………………………57

41. Dialectical materialism
42. Value
43. Religion
44. Free will
45. Humanity's greatest weapon
46. Computer science
47. Martial arts
48. Mixed Martial Arts

49. Confrontation
50. Pacifism

<u>Core principles</u>

Philosophy

In order to live a fulfilling life you must have a good philosophy, because without having your own set of beliefs you can't hope to achieve anything. You must always seek to learn, seek to adapt and seek to think to be always improving your philosophy.

You must also apply your philosophy to unknown situations because through life you will always face new situations you have not seen before, new concepts and so your philosophy must be used so that you can know how to handle the situation and find what the best path forward is.

Adaptation

To be able to achieve anything it is necessary to adapt.

Without adaptation, when we stick to our beliefs because of ego we become stagnant and our beliefs become dogmatic.

It is important to know that people's ideas are usually wrong. Or at least there is usually a little truth to it but the majority of it is incorrect.

That is why we must discuss our beliefs to get a better sense of the truth, because if you have two people with two different philosophies, both of which resemble a small bit of the truth but are highly flawed. Then the people talk and from that conversation they reach a conclusion somewhere in the middle which is closer to the truth and then the action is repeated over and over with other people eventually your philosophy adapts to be closer to the truth. Which is why discussion is extremely important to achieve the truth.

It is important to have an open mind, because an open mind is the only way you can adapt. If you continue to be dogmatic then you achieve anything.

Scientific analysis

Scientific analysis is the best way to get as close to the truth as possible.

What I see a lot of people doing is by not using scientific analysis in order to achieve and instead use common sense.

Common sense is an extremely flawed philosophy for finding truth. This is because common sense ultimately based on personal experience and how you see the world. However how you see the world is not how the world is in different places.

Let me explain, for example if we look at the way people thought about how human health worked. We can see that people used common sense and thought of ideas such as the miasma causing illness.

This was constructed by humans because it was something that can be understood. The idea that bad air is what caused illness.

We know it is germs that cause illness through scientific analysis. Using common sense has on many occasions proved to be wrong and in many situations caused more suffering like how the four humours did.

This is why we must not use common sense to reach our understanding and beliefs. Instead we must use collection of data and scientific analysis in order to reach conclusions, as this has consistently shown to be better at getting the truth.

Criticism

Criticism is extremely important in order to adapt which leads to a better understanding of the world.

A lot of people don't like criticism because criticism makes people feel attacked. It makes us feel like because our beliefs are been criticised it is like we ourselves are been attacked.

However, it is important to distinguish because our philosophy. Our philosophy is always changing and adapting. So in order to adapt we must take criticism as a good thing and as a tool that can be used to improve ourselves.

This is why we must think about issues, as thinking is very important to gain truth, and discuss it with people we disagree with to help get criticism so we can adapt.

Bad criticism: criticism can be bad if the person who is doing the criticising is not doing it well intentioned to help people improve themselves.

How can you know the difference? Bad criticism usually attacks their person rather than the philosophy. For example in a discussion an example of bad criticism is when people start saying stuff like the other person is stupid, starts using logical fallacies or something along those lines.

This criticism must be avoided at all costs, while good criticism is encouraged as it is necessary to help us adapt our philosophy for the better.

Balance

In many situations in life there is not one correct solution. May of the times you must take the goods of different philosophies.

It is very unusual for 1 set path to be 100% correct which is why you must not go for one philosophy, you must take the good from both philosophies and disregard the bad.

It is like in martial arts. All the best Martial artists don't stick to one style they learn a mixture of striking and grappling martial arts. The same can be said about methods of thinking in general. You must find balance if you want to find truth.

New Soviet Man

There was this idea in the USSR of a New Soviet Man the idea of been the best human possible. I believe that we should all strive to have the characteristics of a New Soviet Man. The main characteristics I believe we should promote are:

1. Been educated. We must all strive to learn as much as possible, we should all study and work hard to gain more knowledge as without knowledge we cannot hope to improve ourselves or society.
2. Hard work. A good communist must be hard working, we should always oppose laziness.
3. Be Soviet before any other ethnicity. We should all learn that as humans we are all similar. When we identify as English, Russian, or French we separate ourselves. We put ourselves in this group that not everyone can be a part of. However we must all learn that we are all far more similar than you might think, we are all humans who strive to make the world a better place.
4. Love everyone. We must love everyone as brothers and sisters and forgive them when they make mistakes and help people.
5. 4. Selflessness. A good communist must always be concerned with other's wishes rather than their own and must always peruse justice.

These are some of the characteristics I think a good communist must-have.

Some people only pretend to be a good person. They only work hard when someone is watching and boast about it as much as they can.

This is not a good attitude, people should always work hard and do the right thing all the time even when nobody is watching and should not go around telling people about it because doing the right thing for the sake of been a good person is what it means to be a good person.

So ultimately if you want to be a good person you should be humble and should do your hard work and good actions in private. It is like Bruce Lee said "showing off is the fool's idea of glory."

The meaning of life

Life and happiness

The ultimate meaning of life is to peruse passion and happiness. There is not one ultimate thing for everyone that will give them the full meaning of life.

Instead the meaning of life is something that is different for everyone. This is because humans are all different with their own DNA, which is why we have different passion.

This is why one must seek self-knowledge and find what is it that one is passionate about and wishes to peruse.

The meaning of life is not fame or wealth but it is to peruse happiness and when I mean happiness, I do not mean short term happiness caused by consumerism. I am talking about true happiness or long term happiness. This can be achieved through achieving goals, having a good sense of community and by helping other people.

Ultimately an ordinary person is the most important person on the world. It is not world leaders or billionaires but it is every single person because every single individual person has their own goals and dreams, their own life to live out which is the most important thing.

Yourself

You must find out about yourself as ultimately only you can know what you want and if you struggle to find this out you should not be afraid of asking people for help.

The most important things to do for your self is:

Self-knowledge: knowledge over oneself and what it is that your passions and interests are.

Self-expression: do not be someone who you are not, free yourself by expressing yourself, do what you are passionate about and what you have motivation for.

Self-actualisation: after realising what you want and perusing it you can then achieve what it is that you want to achieve.

Finding what you are motivated for and passionate about and then perusing it is the most important thing because when this is done nothing can stop you in your goals and passion.

Determination and never giving up

The meaning of life is to peruse passion and happiness. To do this you must look at what you want to achieve and achieve it.

On the way you will fail and through hard work you will achieve your goals.

Everyone knows that hard work will beat natural talent when natural talent refuses to work hard.

However, it goes further than this, because the skill and mentality of been determined is far more important than actually reaching the goal in the end. After all "the goal is nothing the movement is everything."

When you have the mentality of been determined to improve in the activity you are passionate about you will work day and night in order to achieve the goal. You will continue to work no matter the amount of times you fail because the idea of failing is so unbearable that no matter what you will keep going.

Even when hard work fails to win it is the greatest success. Because the mindset of picking yourself up after defeat and continuing to work shows character and spirit. You show yourself to be the best version of yourself and is ultimately the final victory that anyone can have.

Failure

Failure, is not necessarily a bad thing. This is because without failure we cannot learn, we cannot adapt.

The only way to succeed is by failing and without failing you won't achieve anything which is just as bad as failing, because ultimately what is worse failing a job interview or not attempting the interview in the first place. In both situations the person did not get the job the only difference is the person who attempted the interview gained more experience on how to improve for the next interview.

Failure is a negative emotion for humans. It makes us sad, however it is nothing to fear. To conquer our goals we must fail and so it is important to always work to the point of failure to improve.

To achieve success it is necessary to always push yourself to the point of failure to go until you can't go any further. By doing this you improve and the more you push yourself to failure the more you will be able to do.

Adversity

Everyone experiences adversity. In the end adversity is a natural experience that everyone experience.

When facing adversity it is usually in attempting to achieve long term happiness. When facing adversity you must be determined to never give up.

In order to learn certain skills you must also face adversity. For example to improve your memory or concentration, both very important skills for success, the only way to improve them is by facing adversity to ultimately achieve your goals.

No matter how hard the situation is you must stay focused and always give it your all, by doing this you will always achieve your goal and overcome all challenges.

Ultimately adversity is not a bad thing it teaches people discipline to face difficult situations and facing adversity leads to long term happiness.

Discipline

Discipline is something that cannot be taught. It is something that one can only give themselves. Once a person learns to discipline themselves and learns to face adversity then they will be fully unstoppable and can achieve anything they want.

Writing to yourself

Writing to yourself is very important because writing to yourself helps you remember ideas and goals.

It is also important to write to yourself in the second person because that way notes can be understood by everyone and it will make you remember it better.

Actions speak louder than words

Actions ultimately speak louder than words because until you can put your words into action the thought of your words becomes ultimately useless.

Words and beliefs are still extremely important. They are important because without the correct methods of thinking our actions can lead to horrific results.

This is why you must find balance. You must always be looking to adapt your theory but you must also practise your theory because without practising and testing your theory you might as well not have that philosophy.

Health

Your body is the most wonderful thing you have. Which is why you must take good care of it.

Do not damage your body and take good care of it. Treat it well, do not poison it.

For some people taking care of their body is much easier than for others. Some people enjoy doing exercise while for others it is a chore. You will have to learn discipline if you do not enjoy if it you want to keep your body in good health.

Doing exercise every day is extremely important to keep your body in good health. You should also rest your body if you are ill or injured because trying to do exercise when that happens will just harm you more.

You should also make sure not to do too much exercise as it is possible to over train which can also be very bad for your health, that is not to say you should not push yourself as you should always push yourself to your limits but when you get to the point where you are fully collapsing and having to go to the hospital because of over training then you should stop as that is also dangerous.

I have found that 25 hours a week of martial arts training is ideal as when I go over that I start getting symptoms of over exhaustion.

For food, only eat what your body requires but also do not starve yourself and eat what it requires to keep yourself in good health,

Then there is stuff that is extremely bad for you such as smoking, drinking and gambling. If you have never started then keep it that way as it will only effect you negatively.

As for sleep, make sure you go bed early so that you get all the sleep you need, do not under sleep or oversleep as balance is necessary.

For others it may be harder to keep good health and it is only when one teaches themselves discipline can they keep good health.

Sometimes they will also need to seek professional advice for how to help do this, never be afraid to change and don't be afraid to ask for professional help.

Peer pressure

You must not allow peer pressure to govern your life. Only do something because you want to do it never do something you don't want to do.

That is not to say you cannot do what people tell you to do. If someone tells you to do something and you want to do it or do not mind to do it then why not do it? It is only when you do something you don't want to do then you are giving into peer pressure.

Do not be influenced by what people think of you, be yourself. If somebody does not love you for who you are then it is them who must change not you.

Some people also submit to peer pressure not because they are embarrassed or care about what people think of them but because they are agreeable people who want to make people happy.

However been an agreeable person does not lead to good success because you give up what is good for you and ultimately if someone wishes for you to not be yourself then they are not worth pleasing.

You need to train yourself to not be agreeable because without doing so you will fail in your goals and won't be able to stand up for yourself.

Ego

A person's ego is one of your greatest enemies because your ego is what causes you to not be adaptive, you can't accept criticism and can't achieve success because it causes you to not face Adversity and to not attempt anything if there is a chance of failure.

To me what I see is a lot of people want to learn to win but don't want to learn to lose. However one cannot win without losing.

In order to reach a fulfilling life one must learn to remove their ego. One does not ever need to want to lose but must not be afraid of losing and when someone stops been afraid of losing they have successfully removed their ego because without the fear of failure one can achieve all their goals.

How can you help someone remove their ego? Unfortunately you cannot help someone overcome their ego because telling someone they have an ego further damages their ego.

Some things you cannot help people with and they must overcome it themselves.

Self-belief

In order to achieve success one must belief in themselves. However one must find balance between believing in themselves and having an ego.

Forming an ego is bad but not believing in yourself is also a problem. This is because without self-belief your mind will believe that you won't be able to achieve and your body is ultimately controlled by your brain meaning that a lack of self-belief leads to you not been able to achieve what you want to achieve.

Knowledge

The ultimate knowledge is knowing how little you know, because there is so much to know nobody can ever know everything which is why people specialise.

We must also learn to adapt, accepting the fact that our beliefs our wrong and we don't know everything so we must always be looking to learn.

Without knowledge you can't ever hope to peruse passion as passion requires knowledge in order to pursue it. Which is why we must always strive to learn more.

Ultimately, humans do not like not knowing which is why when people don't know something they make up stories like religion to explain what they don't know, but this is a bad attitude we must accept that we don't know certain things, but that does not mean we cannot pursue this knowledge, after all the goal is nothing the pursuit is everything.

Attempting to pursue knowledge is more important than having the knowledge because to figure out the truth is what is what gives people enjoyment.

Death

Do not neglect life by focusing on death. If you worry about death you stop focusing on what is important and that is living a full fulfilled.

You must learn to live a life full of no regrets. So when you die you can say I did what I wanted to do and what I've done, I've done with sincerity and to the best of my ability and with that you can live a meaningful life.

We cannot live for ever but acceptance of death is essential for not holding back what you have, because what we have is already something that is meaningful and that is the blessing of life, the freedom to do what we want to do so make the most of it.

Simply, do not wish upon death but do not fear it.

Furthermore some people say that immortality is not something to be wished for. We cannot know this as there hasn't been anyone immortal.

The idea is that without death you lose your passion for what you want to do because you will know you always have the next day to do something the same reason having a deadline for homework makes people do the homework.

With immortality you just get tired, tired of watching everyone you know die and you get tired of the struggle of life and lose all that is meaningful in life without death.

Decline

Everyone always wishes that they could live in their prime forever. However everyone at a certain age begins to lose the abilities they had as the human body begins to die.

However this does not mean that you cannot continue to live a full and meaningful life.

Life is about perusing passion and the ability to continue the things that you love is what allows you to continue to live a fulfilling life. Which is why even after you pass your prime you can still live life to the fullest.

When you go past your prime your experience is also at an all-time high. You have experienced so much and with that experience you learn what your mistakes are and what could have been done differently.

This means that you can continue to teach the next generation and help people to succeed.

<u>Making the world a better place</u>

Empathy

Empathy is ultimately what drives people to want to help people and to be the New Soviet Man. It is part of what makes us humans

Helping others makes us happy because we empathise with others.

When we do something wrong or do not help people we feel guilty, and guilt is one of the worst feelings someone can have.

Morality

Morality is something that is an important matter and an incorrect morality leads to a person instead of helping the people they will end up harming people.

Therefore it is important to know what the best way of distinguishing what is right and wrong.

I believe that the best moral system is that of a collective mindset. The needs of the many outweigh the needs of the few.

If you have the option to save 5 people or save one person, you would save 5 people. This is what is used to decide if a war is justified because you look to see is the war going to save more lives than it kills.

For example the war against the Nazis we know that it saves more lives than it kills so therefore the war is justified while the US invasion of Iraq killed more people than it saved so therefore it is not justified.

However there are a few criticisms of this philosophy. One example is if a majority of people decide to oppress the minority would that be justified. No, because the death of one person does more damage to society than the sadness filled by the people who want the person dead.

You see the collective policy says that the society is the most important thing, this is not the same as what most people want though it is what does more damage to society and overall 1 man's death is worse for society than the happiness the people gain from wanting the one person dead.

The second criticism I see a lot is if the person does not experience the suffering would that make it justified. For example if someone punches while they are under anesthesia would that be justified?

No because the person does not need to experience the pain for the damage to be done to their body so the damage to society is still done. Therefore utilitarianism and collectivist theory still stands as the best way of determining if an action is right or wrong.

Teaching

"Give a man a fish and you feed him for a day. Teach a man to fish and you feed him for a lifetime"

To help people it is important to not only give them what they need but teach them how they can provide for themselves.

Teaching and passing down your knowledge is one of the kindest things you can do to a person because you are not just giving them what they need once or twice but you give them what they need to throughout their whole life. Which is far more important than just giving what they need this one time.

A good teacher should never give up on their students, no matter how bad the student is, the teacher should not tell them they are a failure or even believe their student is a failure believe it, because humans have the super power to transform themselves and achieve anything.

However, if you tell someone they are a failure then they will ultimately believe that they are a failure and will go into this self-fulfilling prophecy that the teacher has set out.

Remember, that we should always adapt so a good teacher should not teach a student what to think but how to think when they learn the method of how to achieve success then they can decide what the best philosophy is. In essence a teacher should be like a sign that shows people the correct path if they are lost and tell them how they could find the right path.

Even these words should be examined by everyone and in the end it is up to each individual to decide what best fits them.

A good teacher must also sometimes not give their student what they want but what is best for them. Sometimes doing what is best for someone is not what they want.

For example, if a child wants to have a second desert, that does not want mean that they should be given it as it is bad for them. This is one of the most important parts of teaching, sometimes in order to be kind you must do something that makes them sad.

Politics

The thing I hate about politics is how much hate grows between politicians. Politicians become corrupt and do bad things to try and gain more power.

Politics is evil and a terrible thing. However it is also necessary to make the world a better place which is why getting involved in politics is essential if you want to make the world a better place.

Overall politics needs to change, the world needs to stop hating and attacking each other and cooperate and love each other, as brothers and sisters.

Utopia

The perfect society, can it be achieved? What is meant by Utopia, because a perfect society is different for everyone? To me a perfect society is a stateless, classless, moneyless society where everyone lives community and each works to their ability and takes what they need.

There are 3 approaches to achieving Utopia. There is the Conservative approach, the Utopian approach and the Scientific approach.

The Utopian approach: this approach is practised by Utopian Socialists and Anarchists. They do not think through the scientific method and are to idealistic.

This is why Utopian Socialism and Anarchism fail because they fail to see that you can't just go straight to Utopia.

The Conservative approach: when I talk about the Conservative approach, I do not mean just right wing conservatives but in terms of people who belief that a Utopia cannot be achieved and therefore we should not try, this basically means any sort of people that support capitalism including liberals and Social democrats.

Conservativism means commitment to traditional values and ideas with opposition to change or innovation. Therefore liberal and social democrats, while a less extreme version of pure conservatives, still oppose change and innovation towards Utopia seeing it as unreachable.

The problem with conservativism is the fact that they give up to easily. They look and see that they can't be achieved right now and so stop trying, they accept the status quo and society remains as horrible as it always was.

The Scientific approach. The Scientific approach finds balance. It sees that going straight to the Utopia is impossible however they do not give up. They continue looking through solutions, they never give up and will never back down.

We must all learn to do this even a task that seems impossible is always solvable as long as we continue to work towards making a better society.

The transition phase

Scientific Socialists understand that going straight to the Utopia is impossible. That is why before we go to communism we must first go through Socialism first.

Socialism is the transitionary period in which the workers control the means of production. Meaning the economy belongs to the people and is working towards communism.

Socialism is achievable right now and to achieve the utopia the right material conditions need to be met.

Now how to get these material conditions you can disagree with, but what I urge everyone to do is to despite disagreeing with the solutions do not give up on the final goal, instead look to improve the solutions in order to achieve Utopia.

Now what I believe needs to be done to achieve Utopia is as follows:

1. To gain a moneyless society we need there to be enough abundance of wealth that anyone can take what they need and we won't run out. This means that we need to have a society where there is enough production to meet people's needs. However the problem isn't really a problem of production but rather of distribution. We

currently produce enough food for 10 billion people but yet people starve, this means that to fix this all that needs to be done is having things equality distributed so that everyone can take what they need not just the people in the first world.

2. Work needs to be optional. This means an end to blackmailing people to have to work because if they don't they won't get any money and will die. We can see from society a lot of people want to work not for money for enjoyments. Because humans are not just motivated by money, they are only motivated by money because that is how society has conditioned them to think. This is why a cultural revolution is needed, it is why we need everyone to want to be like the New Soviet Man.

3. Jobs people are not interested in. There will always be certain jobs that people are not interested in doing. For these jobs they should be done by machines, therefore we will always have what we need and then people who want to work will have the option to do that work for their enjoyment and will not have to stick to one job but can do whatever work they want to do. If they want to be a fisherman one day and a farmer the next they should be able to do that.

4. Classless and stateless, these can only be achieved when the word unites in peace. Only when everyone unites under the flag of humanity, only then can this be achieved and for this we just need people to believe. For everyone to believe in Utopia is the hardest obstacle to overcome for this and this can only be done by talking to people and trying to get people to want to try and achieve the Utopia and then we can.

Meritocracy

Meritocracy, the idea that how hard you work determines how much you get.

The first common misconception is that the world is a meritocracy. The fact of the matter is that we do not, there are people working in sweatshops for 100 hours a day who get barely nothing, how can we call the world a meritocracy when this happens?

Furthermore even within the developed world there is still unfair advantages for people at the top such as inheritance, the fact that to get better education you have to pay money and not to mention the amount of luck that is correlated to people who succeed, this is extremely unmeritocratic.

Also, the idea of meritocracy in the western world is wrong, because what determines what are good jobs? It is the ruling class who ultimately make jobs like doctors or lawyers far more important while people with different abilities are not related as importantly by society.

A farmer contributes to a society just as much as a lawyer does as without farmers we could not eat. So our society has got a very twisted view of what is considered a good job.

Furthermore is meritocracy something that we should hope for? No life should not be seen as a competition where the losers starve to death.

Instead life should be seen as a cooperation between people who wish to help their fellow brothers and sisters.

Meritocracy is still important in the transitional face when we still need money to incentivise work, but not the meritocracy we have. A meritocracy where every member of society is given fair opportunities and people with different passions are treated fairly by society.

Democracy

The problem with democracy is that it wastes too much time talking about the issue instead of getting things done, which is why authoritarian states are more efficient.

It also means that you can't have experts advise as much as someone who specialises in a certain area will know more on how to achieve the best results in that field which is why the Vanguard party is able to govern so effectively because when the class conscious experts govern they know how to develop the lives of the people.

However as Churchill said "democracy is the worst form of government – except for all the others that have been tried."

The one thing democracy is good at is protecting human rights, all the other forms of governments tend to have worse human rights.

This is why we need a democratic chamber and a chamber for experts so for example experts in healthcare can give advice for how to stop pandemics.

However when I mean a democratic system I do not mean the fake democracy we have where we just chose our dictator for the next 5 years.

I mean a true Soviet/Worker's Council democracy. Where people delegate representatives to represent their work place which will be more democratic and stop corruption.

Helping people

I believe that the only way to truly fix problems is through political work. The problem with charity is that it never fixes the problem only makes the problem smaller. The best ways to help do this is by:

1. Organising and cooperation, make sure that you are united as it is far easier to make change united rather than on your own.

2. Either:
    a. Help break the chains of imperialism by supporting working class movements abroad. This will weaken the imperial core and will lead up to revolution.
    b. Try to build class consciousness, through elections, mutual aid, and any form of mass organisation. We need to get the people on our side. Once we have the will of the people no force can stop the liberation of the working class.

Mutual aid is better than simply just charity because mutual aid educates the people and helps them understand why they are in this situation and how they can improve their situation.

You must also not neglect helping people on a small scale which is just as important. Such as helping a friend with shopping or helping parents with shopping.

Making the world a better place is hard because humans are not perfect and no matter how hard anyone tries we will always mess up at some point. Which can be a bit hard to accept because whenever you do something right everyone ignores it and the tiniest things you do wrong you get shouted at.

You see with anyone you know for too long they always take your actions for granted. Which is a good thing. Because it shows that they see you as a reliable person, so when you do something to help them they see that as a normal thing from you and then when you forget something they get really mad.

However, remember as someone wants to make the world a better place whenever you mess up just remember that you have helped someone far more and that is all the satisfaction you need, you don't need any praise because that is not your intentions as long as you know you are doing the right thing, the satisfaction you need.

Initiative

Initiative is very hard to master but is very important to helping people.

Without initiative you cannot hope to help people because to help someone one must think for themselves what can be done to help people.

Many of the times you will not know what to do and the only way to improve this is by facing adversity and to keep trying.

You will also sometimes do the wrong thing when you think you are doing the right thing and again the only way to get better at knowing what the best action is to help someone one must simply keep trying and eventually you will improve.

Mass line

The mass line, is a very important principle to hep improving the world.

The idea is that you go to the people to see what need and see what they want and implement what they want. This is very important because while we ore selves can never fully know what the people want, only the people can know what they want and so to help the people we need to know what the people want and so we must follow the principles of mass line to make the world a better place.

Mistaken ideas and correct ideas

Middle man fallacy

A middle man fallacy is when someone uses balance to unbalance.

A middle man fallacy occurs when a person says their view is justified just because it is in-between two extremes.

Balance is only good when you look at to theories and both have good in them because sometimes one extreme might not have flaws and to disregard parts of it just for the sake of finding balance is not finding balance it unbalances an already balanced theory.

In essence it is important to balance your beliefs because you take the goods from two opposing philosophies but you must not find balance for the sake of finding balance otherwise this takes away the point of finding balance.

Existence

"Sum, ergo cogito", "I think therefore I am" we know we exist even though we don't know if what we are experiencing is the true experience we know that there is some sort of existence.

What might that reality be? Well for that we have no way of knowing. It might be that we are having a dream, or trapped in a simulation but we simply have no way of knowing and to say we don't know is much better that making beliefs with no evidence.

Similar to if Gods exist, we have no way of knowing so it is best to say we do not know rather than having made up beliefs and stop searching for the answers.

What really does exist? This might seem obvious to the world we see around us but in worlds we cannot see, they do not follow the physics that is normal for us and so we chose not to believe it.

For example in Quantum mechanics there is a concept called wave-particle duality. Under this concept a quantum entity may be either a particle or a wave. Now think about how crazy that is, imagine if every object you can see, you, your house or your car could be either a particle or a wave. It would mean your house could become a wave.

The philosophy of physics tries to understand what is actually their? Because what we observe is so unheard and does not happen in our world that we do not understand it.

For this it is important to stick to the scientific method. What exists is what we observe and using common sense to say wave-particle duality does not exist is the wrong approach to understanding what exists.

Time

What is time? Time is a very hard thing to define. Is time the passing of events? Or the overseer of the events of the universe?

Perhaps but remember that time is relative, we know that the stronger the gravity the more space-time curves, this means the close you get to an object with a big mass the more your time slows down and getting close enough time stops completely. Essentially if someone saw you falling into a black hole you would fall slower and slower until you just froze completely.

The same happens with speed, the faster you go you slow down and as you approach the speed of light time stops completely.

So time is the passing of events, but it is relative to every object so it is your very own passing of events as it changes for every object depending on different factors.

However, while time is relative while on Earth we can only go forward at 1 hour per hour, we cannot reach the speed of light and can't go to a black hole so for us time remains in the past, present and future.

This means we cannot change the past and the future has not happened yet. Therefore only focus on what is now, do everything now to your best ability. Do not worry about the past because you can't change it, do not worry about the future as that has not happened yet. You are you know and that is all the matters.

Learn from the mistakes in the past to make the actions in the present the best actions possible and use the present to make the future as bright as possible.

Nostalgia

Nostalgia is a powerful feeling that can both make us happy and make us sad that the good times are gone.

In the end we should not be sad that good things are gone we should be happy that they happened.

We have the ability to change our present and so you can use the past to determine the best course of actions in the present to achieve more good things.

As for the things that are gone we can remember them and make them a part of us so in the end good things don't really have to come to an end, they become a part of us.

Forgiveness

We cannot change the past and so the mistakes you done in the past cannot be changed. Therefore we must always forgive each other, because even the worst person can change if they really want to.

Therefore a changed person, should not be judged on what they have done as they are a different person in what they do and so must have the same treatment as everyone else.

After someone apologises and is trying to do the right thing do not make them feel more guilty about it, as guilt is one of the worst feelings someone can have and nobody deserves to have someone damaging their self-belief constantly after they have changed their ways.

To forgive someone else is easy but one must learn to also forgive oneself. When you make a mistake you feel guilty and you feel that you wish you could go back and change what you have done. The amount of guilt and torture people put on themselves is so unbelievable.

Many people forgive other people forgive other people easier than they forgive themselves. However, you must also learn to forgive yourself as it has just as bad negative effects on yourself as it would on anyone else.

It damages your self-belief as the more you tell yourself you are a horrible person the more you will believe you are a horrible person and will ultimately believe what you tell yourself so you must learn to forgive yourself.

Respect

Respect everyone, no matter what their social class is, if they are the head of state or a bin man you should treat everyone equally.

People have a tendency to give more respect to people who have higher rankings in society. However, everyone is just as valuable to society and nobody should be discriminated against.

You must always respect everyone you meet, be polite and kind to everyone.

Do not think you are better than anyone, you must always be willing to learn from everyone, because each individual is filled with knowledge.

Everyone has lived through life and has had so much experience and has gained so much knowledge. This is why you must be willing to learn from anyone because everyone has useful knowledge.

Do not let your ego stop yourself from learning. Everyone must learn to remove their ego as the ego is one of your greatest everyone. Treat everyone with equal respect because everyone is equally valuable to society.

Control

One must learn control, because having great power without been able to control that power is worse than not having the power at all.

Controlling one's emotion as well is just as important as controlling power because without controlling emotions you will cause harm just like not controlling power.

Emotion

We have to find balance between emotion and logic.

If you become purely logical you become a psychopath with no emotion and no meaning.

However acing based on pure emotion is also flawed as it means you do not make the best decision.

Emotions have helped humans survive. All emotions even bad emotions such as sadness as without sadness we would not know what situations are bad so all emotions are necessary.

However, you need to also control your emotion and to not act based of emotion.

<u>Different philosophies</u>

Dialectical materialism

Dialectical materialism is one of the most important things for Marxists to understand.

It states that historical events result from the conflict of social forces and are interpretable as a series of contradictions and their solutions with these conflicts been caused by material needs.

If we look at history we can see this is quite commonly the case for example the French Revolution been the result of contradictions between what the Aristocracy and the people's wants based on their material needs.

This is crucial to understand to get a good sense of the causes of historical events.

Value

What determines value? There are to theories to help explain this:

The labour theory of value: this theory states that value is determined by the materials used to produce it + the work done by the worker. E.G. the value of a smart phone is determined by the value of the materials used to build it E.G. the screen of it + the work done to get those materials, design it and build the phone.

The subjective theory of value: this states that the value is determined by supply and demand, the more demand there is for a product the more valuable it is and the amount that can be supplied also determines the value of a product.

I believe that the labour theory of value is the correct theory for value. The subjective theory of value describes more on price. Price and value are different.

The value of something that never changes and stays the same while the price is the value but adjusted for supply and demand.

Religion

The main problems I have of religion is that it has no scientific proof behind it, it is based on faith and common sense. While without scientific analysis we know it ultimately leads to terrible mistakes.

The second problem is that it becomes dogmatic, because to believe in religion you must believe the Holy Book. However the Holy Book has flaws such as what the Abrahamic Religion says about how the world was created in 7 days or how homosexuals are not seen as equals.

There are to approaches to how people following religion can have to this. Either they can change their mind on what is said in the Holy Book, but in that case you are deviating from the religion, because to believe in religion means you should have undeniable faith in what is said so a Christian must have faith in the Bible, or a Muslim must have faith in the Quran, because if one part of the Holy Book is wrong how do you know that not all of it is wrong.

If one stays true to all of the belief. Well in that case it proves my point, that religion is dogmatic as it cannot be adapted and analysing the Bible or the Qur'an we can see massive flaws, so if there is a God that is Omnibenevolent they would not have said all those things to have been said. If there is a God that does believe in mistreatment of homosexuals, then this God is not omnibenevolent and must not be followed. If this God is followed than that is a mistaken idea and the only reason for those beliefs is because of a dogmatic text.

Free will

Free will is the power of acting without the constraint of fait holding you back. Free will is something humans have, the conscious choice of deciding what we want.

However, how much events are truly determined by free will rather than events. The conscious part of the brain is a very small part of making decisions and ultimately a lot of things such as choosing what your favourite food is ultimately not up to free will.

However the problem with determinism is that it has many of the flaws that most doctrines have and that is the fact that they only get part of it right.

Humans have the ability to decide our action even if it goes against what the unconscious part of the brain is telling us to do is. Such as when people fast their subconscious part of the brain tells them to eat but the person does not or what about when there is no want and it is just 2 random boxes for you to choose from. Free will still has an important part in our society and determines many events.

Humanity's greatest weapon

"The pen is mightier than the sword" ultimately a person's voice is the most dangerous weapon one can have.

Your voice can be used to stop discrimination like how Martin Luther King helped stop discrimination against black people in the US.

However, your voice just like all weapons can be used for bad things, like how Hitler killed millions of people by using his voice to rally the nation behind him.

Without a voice you won't be able to find the confidence to defend yourself and it is through your voice that you inspire people behind a cause which can be either good or bad.

Computer Science

People think that computer science is about making computers, but it goes further than that. Computer Science and computational thinking is a way of thinking that can be applied to outside computers.

Thinking like a computer scientist means thinking through everything logically, like a computer.

It is used for software development and making computers because computers are logical and need everything explained and that same logic can be used outside of technology to solve problems as well.

Martial arts

Martial arts has changed a lot over years. Originally it was designed as a way of self-defence. However it has evolved to become more of a sport.

This is because our society has advanced. Crime is so less prevalent than it was when martial arts was made because as society develops crime gets lower, meaning a lower need for self-defence.

Furthermore technology has also increased, now if you face someone with a gun no amount of martial arts can save you from a gun.

However, martial arts has not died out it has only adapted, while still putting a lot of focus on self-defence it has adapted to become more than just self-defence. It has become more of a sport and martial arts has always been and always will be a way to help improve the lives of its practitioners.

Martial arts becoming more of a sport is not necessarily bad thing as now you can train your martial arts to become the best possible martial artist you can be and see your progress against other people without anyone getting hurt, as that is what martial arts is about it is for, self-improvement.

Train every part of your martial art, do not just stick to one style as different martial arts have different things to teach and to be a good martial artist you must train every part of your body and all the skills that can be done with it to make yourself the best martial artist you can be.

This is ultimately what Bruce Lee was trying to teach, by forming Jeet Kune Do however Jeet Kun Do has also become a style, a style that focuses on not using a style but still a style, because ultimately it became a mix of martial arts that Bruce Lee studied and became a style that expressed the way of Bruce Lee.

As Bruce Lee said "Do not go out and look for a successful personality and duplicate it" simply you must not try to be someone else, you are only yourself so be yourself, you must find your own version of Jeet Kun Do that expresses yourself by learning from others.

Mixed Martial Arts

I love the idea of MMA. How it combines all sorts of martial arts, this to me has always been a positive thing. However, despite this, I am still against MMA.

This is because I don't believe MMA focuses enough on the control of strikes. To me, the objective of martial arts should not be to try to knock your opponent down and hit them as hard as you can. Instead you need to control because that way you show you have the skill to have hurt them if you wanted to but you have the skill not to.

Control is a very important aspect of martial arts which MMA does not address. I believe MMA should be reformed, or a different sport similar to MMA can be made, one where the control of the martial artist is also assessed.

I do not want to do MMA, because I do not believe there is any need to hurt anyone, to me hurting others is not what martial arts is about.

Confrontation

Confrontation can be good or bad, most of the times it is bad but in a few situations it is good.

For example you must confront yourself to adapt and improve on your mistakes.

However, confronting someone else must be avoided at all cost and should only be done as a last resort.

You should only confront them if not doing so will cause more harm than good.

Challenges: people who challenge someone to a fight have a mistaken mindset and people who accept challenges to a fight are also wrong. This is because the only motive to these challenges is because the people in the challenge are insecure about themselves and are letting their ego control them.

Remember no matter if you win or lose both results are worse than not accepting the fight. You should not care about what people think of you and you should not allow your ego to come before doing what is right, and to do what is right is to not hurt others.

Pacifism

The problem with pacifism is they believe there is never a need for confrontation or violence when it is needed.

For example in WW2 when the Nazi's began invading everywhere, the pacifist ideology states that the Nazi's must have been dealt with peacefully.

However, this would not have worked trying to do so would have got you and everyone you love killed.

Sometimes in order to help people it is necessary to use actions that are considered bad because without doing so you cause more harm than good.

Printed in Great Britain
by Amazon

82655568R00042